Biblical Foundation 5

Living in the
Grace of God

by Larry Kreider

House To House Publications
Lititz, Pennsylvania USA

Living in the Grace of God

Larry Kreider

Updated Edition © 2002, Reprinted 2003, 2005
Copyright © 1993, 1997, 1999
House to House Publications
11 Toll Gate Road, Lititz, PA 17543
Telephone: 800.848.5892
Web site: www.dcfi.org

ISBN 1-886973-04-0
Design and illustrations by Sarah Sauder

C O N T E N T S

Books in this Series

This is the fifth book in a twelve-book series designed to help believers to build a solid biblical foundation in their lives.

A corresponding *Biblical Foundations for Children* book is also available.

Introduction

The foundation of the Christian faith is built on Jesus Christ and His Word to us, the Holy Bible. This twelve-book *Biblical Foundation Series* includes elementary principles every Christian needs to help lay a strong spiritual foundation in his or her life.

In this fifth Biblical Foundation book, *Living in the Grace of God,* we discover that it is grace that motivates God to offer us salvation even though we did not earn it. In fact, we cannot earn it; it is a gift. Our salvation comes as a gift of God's grace, and it can be accessed by our response of faith. God's grace is present in our lives to save us—"the free unmerited favor of God on the undeserving and ill-deserving." Then we will look at the other side of God's grace which is defined as "the power and desire to do God's will." The grace of God is literally "divine energy" that the Holy Spirit releases in our lives. God has given us supernatural provision to live a victorious life. God gives us an abundance of grace! We do not deserve any of it, but the Lord pours it on us anyway!

In this book, the foundation truths from the Word of God are presented with modern day parables that help you easily understand the basics of Christianity. Use this book and the other 11 *Biblical Foundation* books to lay a solid spiritual foundation in your life, or if you are already a mature Christian, these books are great tools to assist you in discipling others. May His Word become life to you today.

God bless you!

Larry Kreider

How to Use This Resource

Personal study

Read from start to finish as an individual study program to build a firm Christian foundation and develop spiritual maturity.

* Each chapter has a key verse excellent to commit to memory.
* Additional scriptures in gray boxes are used for further study.
* Each reading includes questions for personal reflection and room to journal at the end of the book.

Daily devotional

Use as a devotional for a daily study of God's Word.

* Each chapter is divided into 7-day sections for weekly use.
* Additional days at the end of the book bring the total number of devotionals to one complete month. The complete set of 12 books gives one year's worth of daily devotionals.
* Additional scriptures are used for further study.
* Each day includes reflection questions and a place to write answers at the end of the book.

Mentoring relationship

Use for a spiritual parenting relationship to study, pray and discuss life applications together.

* A spiritual father or mother can easily take a spiritual son or daughter through these short Bible study lessons and use the reflection questions to provoke dialogue about what is learned.
* Read each day or an entire chapter at a time.

Small group study

Study this important biblical foundation in a small group setting.

* The teacher studies the material in the chapters and teaches, using the user-friendly outline provided at the end of the book.

Taught as a biblical foundation course

These teachings can be taught by a pastor or other Christian leader as a basic biblical foundation course.

* Students read an assigned portion of the material.
* In the class, the leader teaches the assigned material using the chapter outlines at the end of the book.

CHAPTER 1

What is Grace?

Grace affects everything

A famous zoo in Germany purchased a great brown bear from the traveling circus. Up until this point, this magnificent, but abused creature had lived in misery. For the duration of its life the bear had been locked up in a tiny circus cage about twelve feet long. Every waking hour of the day, with its massive head swaying back and forth in rhythm, he took twelve steps forward and twelve steps backward in his narrow prison. The water given to him was stagnant slop; the food was rotten garbage.

Finally he was sold and transferred from his tiny little cage to the beautiful German Zoo. The zoo had a bear compound consisting of acres of lush, green grass. There were trees to climb and sparkling pools of fresh drinking water. The bear would be fed three meals each day and have other bear companions.

The zoo-keepers wheeled the bear's cage into the compound of the zoo and opened the door to freedom. The bear continued his march—twelve feet forward and twelve feet backward. They called out to him, but he would not respond. They offered him food. They offered him freedom, but he still would not respond.

Finally, the only solution left was to put some rags on a stick, soak them in kerosene, light them and place the burning rags through the bars. This scared the bear enough to jump from the cage onto the ground. The bear looked around, and to the zoo attendant's amazement, he started pacing twelve feet forward and twelve feet backward—the exact dimensions of his cage!

Suddenly it dawned on the attendants—the bear's prison was not a *metal* one, but a *mental, invisible* one! They could do nothing to help him out of his prison and finally had to put him to sleep.

Some Christians find themselves in a similar dilemma. Having become so accustomed to certain thought patterns of defeat and failure in some areas of their lives, they convince themselves things will never change and are locked in an invisible, mental prison.

Precious, born again, Spirit-filled Christians who love Jesus with all of their hearts are susceptible to this kind of mental trap. Some, upon facing incredible obstacles in their lives, become weary and settle for far less than the Lord intended for them.

Years ago, I received a revelation from the Lord about the grace of God that has literally revolutionized my life. Although I was in love with Jesus and filled with the Holy Spirit, I was still living in a mental prison. It seemed like some things would never change. Then one day someone vividly described the "grace of God" to me in a way that literally changed my life! God's grace offered in the scriptures goes far beyond what is offered by other world religions. Many religions say that man gets what he deserves. Others add that man does not get all that he deserves (mercy). Grace goes way beyond that idea, however. Grace is God's unimaginable and total kindness! We receive it freely and do not deserve it, and our hearts cannot but change because of it! We cannot fully describe it, but we can experience it. Grace affects everything we do in life. When I finally began to understand the grace of God, it changed the way I thought, acted and responded to difficulties that arose in my life.

Grace is mentioned more than 125 times in the New Testament. Since "grace" is mentioned so often, we need to understand what the grace of God is really about and how it affects our lives. Paul, the apostle, while writing to the church, often began his letters speaking about grace. He would also close his letters with, "The grace of the Lord Jesus be with you." He continually emphasized *grace* throughout the New Testament. *Grace and peace to you from God our Father and the Lord Jesus Christ. I always thank God for you because of his grace given you in Christ Jesus (1 Corinthians 1:3-4).*

REFLECTION
Like the bear in the cage, are you held captive to any old habits or deceptions?

God's free gift of grace is the basis of salvation

DAY 2

Grace is sometimes defined as *the free unmerited favor of God on the undeserving and ill-deserving.* God loves us and does not want us to be separated from Him by sin. So our first glimpse of grace occurs when God offers salvation to us even though we do not deserve it or work to earn it. He gives a measure of grace as a gift to unbelievers so they may be able to believe in the Lord Jesus. Ephesians 2:8-9 says, *For it is by grace you have been saved, through faith—and this not from yourselves, it is the gift of God— not by works, so that no one can boast.*

We come to God initially because He is the One who has drawn us. Jesus says in John 6:44, *No one can come to Me unless the Father who has sent me draws him.* I've met people who have said, "I found

God." We do not find God; He finds us! He has been drawing us to Himself all along. The reason that we are Christians is simply because of God's grace and God's goodness on our lives. Grace is dependent on the infinite goodness of God. Because of the grace of God—because of His love, goodness and caring as He draws us to Himself, we are saved. We don't deserve to be saved but God freely extends His grace to us. Romans 11:6 says, *And if by grace, then it is no longer by works; if it were, grace would no longer be grace.*

It is grace that motivates God to offer us salvation even though we did not earn it. We cannot earn it; it is a gift. So we see that our salvation comes as a gift of God's grace, and it can be accessed by our response of faith.

Grace could be described as a coin with two distinct sides to it. We just described the one side of the coin that is characterized by the saving grace of God—"the free unmerited favor of God on the undeserving and ill-deserving." The other side of the grace coin is the grace God gives to believers to give them the "desire and the power to do God's will." We will look at this aspect of grace a bit later in this book. Both aspects of grace encompass the whole of the Christian life from the beginning to the end. We are totally dependent on the grace of God!

REFLECTION
How does grace first impact our lives according to Ephesians 2:8-9? Describe the two sides of grace.

Mercy vs. grace

DAY 3

There is a difference between God's grace and mercy. Sometimes we get these two terms confused. God's *mercy* is "God not giving us what we deserve" and God's *grace* is "giving us those things that we do not deserve."

We deserve hell, sickness, disease and troubles because our sin places us in darkness. Yet, even though we do not deserve it, God offers us forgiveness, peace, eternal life, hope, healing, the Holy Spirit: the list goes on—all because of His wonderful grace!

A few years ago, I was traveling through a small town in the Midwest with my family. I was not aware the speed limit was 25 miles per hour and I was traveling 35 miles per hour. As I got to the other side of the town, I heard a shrill siren behind me. Sure enough, it was a policeman, signaling me to pull off to the side of the road. He then proceeded to write up a traffic ticket as he fulfilled his responsibility as a police officer. Now, if the policeman would have been exercising mercy he would have said, "Look, I understand you didn't realize you were going 10 m.p.h. over the limit. I'll allow you to go free." If he would have been operating in a principle of grace, he would have said, "You are a really nice guy. In fact, I like you so much I'd like to give you a hundred dollars just for traveling on our streets." Unfortunately for me, he did not operate in mercy or grace, but he did allow me to receive *justice*—he gave me a ticket with a fine to pay!

I can remember, early in my Christian life, that I felt like God somehow owed me a nice family and a prosperous life, complete with a paycheck each week. After all, I thought, I had worked for it. I didn't realize how arrogant I was. If it wasn't for the grace of God, I would not have the physical strength or health to work in the first place. God didn't owe me anything. First He had shown mercy to me and saved me, then He showered His grace on me, giving me those things I did not deserve—God's wonderful

REFLECTION

What are some things God gave you because of His grace? What are some things He did not give because of His mercy?

presence in my life through Jesus Christ. *Christ Jesus came into the world to save sinners—of whom I am the worst. But for that very reason I was shown mercy so that in me, the worst of sinners, Christ Jesus might display his unlimited patience as an example for those who would believe on him and receive eternal life* (1 Timothy 1:15-17).

No longer under the law but under grace

God gave Moses moral laws to follow (the Ten Commandments) that were given to show men their sinful condition. The law showed the human race the difference between right and wrong. Through attempting to obey the law, mankind sought to earn the blessing of God by what they did.

Then Jesus came and changed all that. Through Him we are offered grace—the free, undeserving favor of God that comes through faith in Jesus, who is the Truth. When a person trusts Christ for salvation, his righteousness no longer depends on keeping the law. Since the Christian is under grace, he cannot be under the law. The Bible says that grace and truth came through Jesus Christ. *For the law was given through Moses; grace and truth came through Jesus Christ (John 1:17).*

Those under the law are always conscious of the power of sin within themselves, frustrating them to live victoriously. Those observing the law must observe all its requirements at all times because if they break even one point, they break the whole law (James 2:10). We cannot become righteous from keeping the law, in fact, it is impossible to keep the law. We all stand self-condemned because we fall short of obeying the law. The only escape is to come out from under the law. That is why we are righteous only by faith in Christ. To escape the dominion of sin, a Christian comes out from under the law and comes under grace. *For sin shall not be your master, because you are not under law, but under grace (Romans 6:14).*

> **REFLECTION**
> *The law came through Moses, but what came through Jesus Christ according to John 1:17? How do we escape the law and come under grace?*

DAY 5

The Ten Commandments show how important grace is

Let's take a brief look at the Ten Commandments (Deuteronomy 5:6-21) to see how far every person falls short of keeping the law. The law helps us to see how important grace is to our lives.

1. **You shall have no other gods before me.**
   We break this law every time we give something or someone other than God complete first place in our affections. No man has ever kept this commandment.
2. **You shall not make for yourself a graven image.**
   It is impossible for an image or picture of God to truly represent God and all His glory. If we approach God with our lips, but not our hearts, we have a false image of Him and are far from Him (Mark 7:6).
3. **You shall not take the name of the Lord your God in vain.**
   Most times we think of using the Lord's name in a profane utterance as "taking His name in vain." But if we call Him *Lord*

and disobey Him, we are taking His name in vain. If we are filled with fear and doubts, we deny His name.

4. **Remember the sabbath day, to keep it holy.**
God's plan was to give man a day of rest so he could worship, undistracted. Christ takes our burdens and gives us a spiritual rest or "Sabbath-rest" (Hebrews 4:10) but often we fail to enter into that rest.

5. **Honor your father and your mother.**
Parents represent God's authority to their children. Yet children are often disrespectful and ungrateful to their parents.

6. **You shall not kill.**
Jesus said that to be angry with another without a cause, and to be insulting, are just as serious as murder (Matthew 5:21-22). We can murder others by gossip, neglect, cruelty or jealousy.

7. **You shall not commit adultery.**
This commandment not only includes sex outside of marriage, but such sin as entertaining adulterous thoughts, looking at pornography, submitting to impure fantasies, selfish demands in marriage, flirting, etc. (Matthew 5:27-28).

8. **You shall not steal.**
Evading income tax is stealing. Working short hours for an employer is stealing. An employer who underpays his workers steals from them.

9. **You shall not bear false witness against your neighbor.**
This is not only referring to what could happen in a court of law, but includes all kinds of idle talk, lies, exaggerations, gossip or even making jokes at another's expense.

10. **You shall not covet.**
Covetousness happens in the heart and mind. When we are jealous of someone's house or life-style or spouse or car, we are enslaved to covetousness.

The Ten Commandments convince us of our sinfulness and inability to keep the righteous law of God. As important as the Ten Commandments are, we simply cannot keep these rules on our own. We need a Savior. Jesus came as the remedy for our sin! Sin does not have dominion over Christians because we are not under the law! We are under grace!

REFLECTION
Think about your life and your inability to keep the Ten Commandments. How important is grace to your life?

Grace is more powerful than sin

God's moral law, the Ten Commandments, are important because they show mankind the true nature of sin. When we see the extent of our failure to obey God's laws, the more we see God's abounding grace forgiving us! The Bible says...*but where sin increased, grace increased all the more (Romans 5:20).*

Grace is much more powerful than sin! Verse 21 goes on to say that sin used to rule over all men and bring them to death, but now God's kindness rules instead, giving us right standing with God and resulting in eternal life through Jesus Christ. Wherever you find sin and disobedience, you will find God's grace available.

The Holy Spirit works within believers to allow them to live lives of righteousness. This is a fulfillment of God's moral law. We cannot do it on our own, but only by God's grace. So grace and obedience to God's law are not in conflict. They both point to righteousness and holiness. We are able to live holy lives and keep God's moral codes only by His grace!

Many years ago, I drove a little Volkswagen "bug." One day, the car stopped running. I decided I had enough of a mechanical background to enable me to take the motor out and fix it. I soon realized that I was getting nowhere fast. I certainly was trying, but I knew I needed help. I towed it to a garage where a mechanic fixed it! Without the grace of God, we cannot fix ourselves. Did I deserve to have the Volkswagen fixed? No, but it ran again because of God's grace and because of the grace on the mechanic who fixed it. It is God's grace that saves us from sin and puts us back together.

If we make a mistake, we confess it to God and move ahead by the grace of God, knowing that it's His grace that gives us the strength to go on. Why did God forgive us? He forgave us because of His gift of grace. Why does God fill us with the Holy Spirit? We're filled because of the grace of God. Even if we have made a mess of our lives, we can find forgiveness and move on because of the grace of God.

REFLECTION
What increases with sin, according to Romans 5:20? How have you experienced this in your life?

Cheap grace?

If God is willing to forgive sin, and since Christians are under grace and not the law, does this mean we can continue to tolerate sin in our lives and yet remain secure from judgment? After all, God's grace pardons sin. We can sin because God will always forgive us, right? Wrong! This is the very issue the early church ran into. Paul challenges this train of thought that "cheapens" God's grace. *What shall we say, then? Shall we go on sinning so that grace may increase? By no means! We died to sin; how can we live in it any longer? (Romans 6:1).*

It is a distortion of God's grace to think we can continue to live in sin and God's grace will cover it. The Bible tells us in 1 John 3:4 that *everyone who sins breaks the law, in fact, sin is lawlessness.* When we came to Christ, we made a separation from sin—we died to sin's power and control over our lives. As Christians, we are freed from sin's power to walk in newness of life (Romans 6:4-5,10). We are no longer slaves to sin.

Yet, every believer must be careful to daily reaffirm his decision to resist sin and follow Christ (Romans 8:13; Hebrews 3:7-11). Known sin in our lives grieves the Holy Spirit and quenches His power (Ephesians 4:30; 1 Thessalonians 5:19). If we keep returning to sin and cease to resist it, eventually our hearts will grow hard and unyielding. It is possible (because of the hardening that can take place in our hearts because of sin—see Hebrews 3:8), we could reach a place in the downward spiral of rebellion and disobedience when we no longer really believe in anything. We become sin's slave again with death as its result. *For the wages of sin is death... (Romans 6:23).*

Although God's grace gives us power to resist sin, it is true that while living our day-to-day lives, we will not always consistently resist sin. When we fail, our God of grace and mercy is willing to forgive us. When we mess up our lives and go back to God, God's grace is freely extended. However, we should be cautioned against thinking we can sin *because* we are under grace. Remember, there may be a point of no return.

REFLECTION
Since grace increases with sin, can we continue to sin because God will always forgive us? What can happen if we keep returning to sin, according to Romans 6:23?

CHAPTER 2

Responding to God's Grace

KEY MEMORY VERSE

But by the grace of God I am what I am,
and his grace to me was not without effect.
No, I worked harder than all of them—yet not I,
but the grace of God that was with me.
1 Corinthians 15:10

Totally dependent on God's grace

Paul, the apostle, went through years of theological training and had an impeccable background of pure Jewish descent. Yet he says that all his advantages of birth, education and personal achievement can be attributed to the grace of God. *But by the grace of God I am what I am, and his grace to me was not without effect. No, I worked harder than all of them—yet not I, but the grace of God that was with me (1 Corinthians 15:10).*

If we think we are strong spiritually or a fantastic husband or a good student or a mature single, we must remember our strength is not in ourselves, but in Jesus Christ. Like Paul, we are totally dependent on the grace of God. Everything that we have, everything that we will ever do, everything that we are, is simply by the grace of God.

When we understand how grace works in our lives, we will find ourselves living with a new freedom in our daily relationship with Jesus. Every good thing in our lives is a result of the grace of God. You and I really do not deserve anything. If you have good health today, it is because of the grace of God. Any gift or ability you have can be credited to the grace of God. If you are an excellent parent, it is not because you are so talented with children, but it is the grace of God that enables you to be a good parent. If you are a fantastic basketball player, it's because of the grace of God. You may say, "But I practice." Who gave you the ability and health to practice? God did. Good students are recipients of the grace of God. If you are a financially secure businessman, the grace of God is the reason that you are successful. When we get this truth into our spirits and live out the grace of God, it totally revolutionizes us. It changes us from the inside out.

The devil cannot puff you up with pride if you understand the grace of God. People who are proud are really saying, "I am the reason things are working so well" and they look to themselves instead of to God. People who are living in the grace of God are always looking to Jesus. They are living with a sense of thankfulness, knowing that He's the One who has given them every good gift and every good thing they have.

REFLECTION

Can you honestly agree with the following statements? I am totally dependent on the grace of God. I am what I am by the grace of God.

God gives us unlimited grace to change

Sometimes people confuse the grace of God with fatalism. Fatalism is the idea that we cannot change our circumstances despite what we do, so we just allow fate to take its course. Although we are totally dependent on the grace of God, it does not mean we sit passively and do nothing to utilize grace. Grace must be diligently desired and accepted.

Imagine yourself lying in the sunshine on a grassy hill on a warm summer's day. A huge rock begins to roll down the hill towards you. Fatalism says, "There's nothing I can do about it. Being crushed by this rock must be my destiny." The grace of God says, "I do not have to just lie here and be crushed by a rock. I will accept and utilize the strength God has given me, and I will get out of its way!" Of course, there are things in life that we cannot change, but we must realize that if it wasn't for the grace of God, things could be much worse. Many undesirable things that happen in our lives can be avoided when we take God at His Word and trust His grace to give us the wisdom and strength to see things changed. God wants to give us more and more of His grace to live victorious as Christians on this earth...*he gives us more grace...(James 4:6)*. At every turn, God is on the lookout to offer grace to us!

Responding in the grace of God always brings more freedom, hope, refreshment and peace so we can move ahead with God. Paul, the apostle, told a church of new believers to continue on in the grace of God even when they had opposition. *Now when the congregation had broken up, many of the Jews and devout proselytes followed Paul and Barnabas, who, speaking to them, persuaded them to continue in the grace of God (Acts 13:43).*

REFLECTION

Describe a time you received grace to live victoriously.

Paul knew that this recently established church of new believers had to have a clear understanding of grace in order to continue to move ahead in His purposes. Otherwise they would succumb to the tactics of the devil and forget that God's grace was sufficient.

Falling short of God's grace

Jesus told a parable one day about a landowner who had a vineyard (Matthew 20:11-15). The grapes were ready to pick, so the landowner found some willing workers and sent them out at 9:00 AM to pick grapes. Later, he hired some more men and sent them out at 12:00 noon. Later still, he employed other workers and sent them out at 3:00 PM. The grape crop was still not completely picked, so at 5:00 PM he sent some final laborers out to complete the harvest for the day. At the end of the day, he called all of the laborers in and gave them exactly the same amount of money because that is what he had promised each group at the start of their job. When the workers who worked the longest hours discovered that the workers who worked only a few hours were paid the same, they complained to the landowner.

If this doesn't sound fair to you, you do not yet understand the grace of God. God loves us unconditionally, just the way we are. When we are secure in His love and acceptance, we no longer are concerned if someone else "gets a better deal" than we do. We live by grace, completely satisfied. When we understand that God's love and acceptance can't be earned or deserved, we live in the blessing of His grace each day.

Did you know that we will never be jealous and become bitter if we understand and live in the grace of God? Hebrews 12:15 says it like this, *See to it that no one misses the grace of God and that no bitter root grows up to cause trouble and defile many.* Bitterness starts out like a small root. Did you ever see a sidewalk where roots had pushed up and cracked the concrete? It started with just one little root. Many times, people get bitter at God. They say, "God, why is that person prosperous and I am struggling financially?" They have fallen short of the grace of God.

REFLECTION
What is a "root of bitterness," according to Hebrews 12:15? Does it ever cause trouble in your life?

1 Corinthians 10:12 says, *So, if you think you are standing firm, be careful that you don't fall!* If we are at the place where we think we are strong and we're going to be okay and we're not going to fall, the Bible says, "Be careful." Any of us can fall short of the grace of God in our lives.

Grace to the humble

There is tremendous spiritual power released when we begin to experience the grace of God. Years ago, I was involved in a youth ministry. I remember coming home one day, and discovering that someone had taken a big rock and thrown it through our window. I knew the rock-thrower was someone we cared about and to whom we had ministered. God was teaching us about His grace, so the Lord helped us to take the attitude that it was only by His grace that our whole house did not have every window broken! We could have cried and complained, but God's grace gave us the power to move on so that we could continue to build His life in the people that He had placed in our lives. 1 Peter 5:5-6 says that...*God opposes the proud but gives grace to the humble. Humble yourselves, therefore, under God's mighty hand, that he may lift you up in due time.*

Humility is an attitude of total dependence on Jesus Christ. Pride is the opposite of a healthy understanding of the grace of God. The scripture makes it clear that if we humble ourselves under the mighty hand of God, He will exalt us in due time. God wants to exalt you. He wants to honor you. When are we honored by God? When we humble ourselves before Him. If I try to do God's job, if I try to exalt myself, then God would have to do my job. He would have to humble me. I would rather humble myself and allow God to exalt me rather than have God humble me, wouldn't you?

Humility places us in a position to receive this grace. True humility is

REFLECTION
According to 1 Peter 5:5-6, how can we humble ourselves?

constantly acknowledging that without Jesus we can do nothing, but with Jesus we can do all things. Humility isn't walking with your head bowed down, trying to look humble. True humility is understanding and living out the principle of the grace of God.

Season your speech with grace

We will not gossip if we understand the grace of God. The reason people gossip is because of false humility. Those who gossip try to elevate themselves on a pedestal as they look down on others. When someone is going through a difficult time or is involved in sin, we may be tempted to gossip about them. We will quickly stop gossiping when we remember that it is only by the grace of God that we are not going through the same things they are experiencing.

The words we speak are very powerful! Words are like dynamite. They can either be used powerfully for good, or they can be used powerfully for evil. *Colossians 4:6* says, *Let your conversation be always full of grace, seasoned with salt, so that you may know how to answer everyone.*

How can we speak with grace, seasoned with salt? When I was growing up, I never liked eating beef liver, but when I got married, I discovered I had a beef-liver-eating wife! One day she served a beautiful meal. The meat smelled and tasted delicious. I said, "Honey, what is this? This meat is really good."

My wife, LaVerne, grinned from ear to ear. "It's liver!" She had seasoned it with the right kind of seasoning, and I liked it.

If you feel like you need to share correction with a struggling person that will help him or her to get back on the right course, season your speech with grace. In other words, say it in a way he or she can receive it. How we say it (with the right attitude) can be as important, if not more important, than what we actually say. Even a word of correction seasoned with grace will tell someone, "I care about you, and you can make it." The Bible tells us to speak the truth in love (Ephesians 4:15).

REFLECTION
Tell about a time you spoke words "full of grace, seasoned with salt" into someone's life. What were the results?

God's grace through suffering

Down through the ages, man has asked the question, "How can God be good and allow us to suffer?" I like the simple answer given by a Nazi concentration camp inmate: "When you know God, you don't need to know why." The important issue is that God is involved in our sufferings. He came and entered our condition—became sin for us, so we might become the righteousness of God (2 Corinthians 5:21).

In fact, God tells us we are to expect suffering (John 16:1-4,33; Titus 3:12). There are many reasons why we suffer—sometimes it is a consequence of our own actions, or because we live in a sinful world, or demonic affliction. If we allow Him to, God will use suffering as a catalyst to spiritual growth in our lives.

Being faithful to God does not guarantee we will be free from trouble or pain in this life. Job, Joseph, David, Jeremiah—the list goes on—all suffered for a variety of reasons. Paul experienced many trials: he was put in chains, and experienced storms and shipwreck. Yet he still proclaimed that no tragedy could "separate us from the love of God" (Romans 8:35-39).

In addition, the Lord will not allow us to be tempted beyond what we can bear (1 Corinthians 10:13). He will provide a way out so that we can stand up under our trials. Our suffering actually opens us up to Christ's abundant grace, according to 2 Corinthians 12:9. *My grace is sufficient for you, for my power is made perfect in weakness....*

In our weakness or suffering, we can count on His strength to make us strong. In our times of tears, troubles, sickness, weaknesses and fears, we can be strong because we have exchanged His strength for our weakness. Our strength comes from His strength, and His alone.

Often, during times of trials and struggles, we find God's grace is very real to us. The Israelites found grace even in the desolate desert. *The people who survived the sword found grace in the wilderness...(Jeremiah 31:2 NKJ).*

God promised to bring good out of our sufferings (Romans 8:28). If we continue to love and obey Him, He will give us the grace necessary to bear our affliction. The Bible says Christians are like "jars of clay" who sometime experience sadness and pain, yet because of the heavenly treasure (Jesus) within, they are not defeated. *But we have this treasure in jars of clay to show that this all-surpassing power is from God and not from us. We are hard pressed on every side, but not crushed; perplexed, but not in despair (2 Corinthians 4:7-8).*

In the midst of all the sufferings and pressures of life, we are sustained by an inner life that cannot be defeated! I have found Jesus to be very close in my life during periods of greatest darkness. Jesus' abundant grace comes in troubled times.

REFLECTION

How does suffering and grace work together, according to 2 Corinthians 12:9?

Allow His grace to motivate you

I used to grumble and think, "God, why do You allow me to experience bad days? I'm serving You. It just doesn't seem right." The Bible tells us, *In everything give thanks, for this is the will of God in Christ Jesus concerning you (1 Thessalonians 5:18).* The Lord is teaching us to give thanks to Him in the midst of bad days. We need to "count our blessings." By God's grace, we have so much for which to be thankful.

One day I was replacing a window in our home. I got frustrated, became careless and broke the window. I realized then that I was trying to put the window in on my strength. I was frustrated and uptight and had moved out of the grace of God. When I admitted, "God, I cannot even put a window pane in without Your grace," do you know what happened? The next window went in with no problem. The grace of God affects even the practical day to day areas of our lives.

Some people love to go shopping. They may get a bargain and think, "This is great. It used to be $35 and I got it for $10! Man, wasn't I lucky?" Not really. It was the grace of God. The world system calls it luck. If you got a bargain while you were shopping, it was simply because of the grace of God on your life. The Lord wants us to thank and glorify Him for His grace to receive bargains! "Good luck" is the world system's replacement for the grace of God.

As a new Christian, I used to wonder why God would let my car break down so often. Now I realize that it was only by the grace of God my old car did not completely quit years earlier! You may ask, "Does God want our cars to break down?" No, of course not, but God wants us, in every situation, to allow His grace to motivate us.

Paul firmly believed that if we receive God's grace and later, by deliberate sin, abandon the faith, we can again be lost. *As God's fellow workers we urge you not to receive God's grace in vain. For he says, "In the time of my favor I heard you, and in the day of salvation I helped you." I tell you, now is the time of God's favor, now is the day of salvation (2 Corinthians 6:1-2).* The grace of God affects us every day! We need to be sure to never take it for granted! As the comic strip character Pogo once stated, "We

REFLECTION
What can happen when we "receive God's grace in vain"? How are we reconciled back to God (2 Corinthians 5:20)?

have met the enemy, and he is us." Only we can block the grace of God from flowing through our lives. If we find ourselves outside the grace of God, we are urged to be reconciled to God (2 Corinthians 5:20). Now is the time to receive His grace and allow it to make a difference in our lives. Let's start today!

CHAPTER 3

Speaking Grace to the Mountain

KEY MEMORY VERSE

"Not by might nor by power, but by my Spirit,"
says the Lord of Hosts. "Who are you, O great
mountain? Before Zerubbabel you shall become
a plain! And he shall bring forth the ca
with shouts of Grace, grace to it!'
Zechariah 4:6-7 NKJ

Grace releases divine energy

In the previous two chapters on grace, we described how God's grace is present in our lives to save us—"the free unmerited favor of God on the undeserving and ill-deserving." Let's focus now on another side of the "grace coin." The other side of God's grace is defined as "the power and desire to do God's will." The grace of God is literally "divine energy" that the Holy Spirit releases in our lives.

Here is a clear example from the scriptures. Zerubbabel was faced with a formidable challenge. When Cyrus the king allowed the Jews to return to their own land, he appointed Zerubbabel to be the governor of the colony. One of Zerubbabel's first responsibilities was to lay the foundation for the new temple. However, due to opposition from the enemies of the Jews, the work on this project soon ceased.

Doesn't that sound familiar? We get a vision from the Lord or begin to take a direction in life and before long we receive opposition and become discouraged and quit. Or maybe we don't quit, but we seem to find it impossible to complete the task that we believe the Lord has laid before us. This is where grace comes in!

One day Zechariah the prophet has a vision from the Lord. As he describes his vision in Zechariah chapter 4:6-7, an angel of the Lord gives Zechariah a prophetic message for Zerubbabel. *"Not by might nor by power, but by my Spirit," says the Lord of Hosts. "Who are you, O great mountain? Before Zerubbabel you shall become a plain! And he shall bring forth the capstone with shouts of Grace, grace to it!" (NKJ)*

The work on the temple was resumed and completed four years later. The Lord gave them "divine energy," and the circumstances supernaturally changed for them to complete the entire project! That which seemed impossible literally happened before their very eyes. They no longer trusted in their own ability, but in the grace of God. As they released divine energy by shouting, "Grace, grace," the *mountain* before them became a *great plain*. They were convinced that the temple was built not by military might, or by political power or human strength, but by the Spirit of the Lord. They had experienced the grace of God!

We can only do God's work if we are enabled by the Holy Spirit. I dare you to apply this scriptural principle to your life. The next time a mountain of impossibility stares you in the face, shout "Grace, grace" to it. See the mountain leveled as you take an act of simple faith and shout "Grace, grace" in the face of the devil. You will find your focus changing from your ability (or lack of ability) to His ability.

Some time ago, I ministered to a group of university student leaders. We stood together and proclaimed "Grace, grace" over every university campus represented at the conference. Faith arose in our hearts as our dependency was no longer in our own strategies and abilities but in the living God.

I find it refreshing to walk into our offices and hear staff persons declaring "Grace, grace" in the midst of deadlines that seem impossible to meet. My faith is increased when fathers proclaim "Grace, grace" over their families. Striving is replaced by a sense of peace and rest in the Lord.

When the children of Israel shouted "Grace, grace" to the temple, they did not sit around and wait for the walls to be built by an angel. They had a renewed sense that, as they worked together fulfilling the plan of God, it was not by their own might or power, but by the Spirit of the Lord that the walls were being built. As we proclaim "Grace, grace" over our lives and situations, we do not receive a license to be lazy. Instead, we receive divine energy to fulfill the purposes of God for our lives.

REFLECTION
Explain "divine energy."
How is it at work in your life?

Speak grace to impossible situations

Skeptics may say, "What does shouting 'Grace, grace' have to do with God acting on our behalf? It seems so foolish." The truth is that the wisdom of God and the wisdom of the world are at odds. *For the message of the cross is foolishness to those who are perishing, but to us who are being saved it is the power of God (1 Corinthians 1:18).*

The wisdom of the world is a wisdom that excludes God and emphasizes our ability to take care of things ourselves. God's wisdom emphasizes a complete dependency on God and His grace. God honors this dependency and obedience to Him.

Why did the army advance only when Moses held up his arms in the battle with the Amalekites? It made absolutely no sense to the natural mind, but Moses was being obedient to his God (Exodus 17).

Jehoash, the king of Israel, came to Elisha, the prophet, for help because the Israelite army faced a massive Aramean army. It seemed like an impossible situation. Elisha instructed King Jehoash to take a bow and some arrows and open the east window. Then Elisha told him to shoot and declared that they would have victory. In addition, the prophet told Jehoash to "strike the ground." The king struck the ground three times and stopped. The prophet Elisha was angry with the king, "You should have struck the ground five or six times; then you would have defeated Aram and completely destroyed it. But now you will defeat it only three times" (2 Kings 13:19). It happened just as the prophet said. King Jehoash showed that he lacked the commitment and faith necessary for the Lord to fulfill His promise. Consequently, he could not completely defeat the Arameans.

What does striking the ground with arrows have to do with winning battles? Nothing, unless the Lord instructs us to do it. In the same way Elisha instructed King Jehoash to strike the ground with arrows, I believe the Lord is calling His people to be obedient and shout "Grace, grace" to situations that seem impossible to them.

REFLECTION
How does God respond to our shouting "grace, grace" to the mountains of impossibility that stare us in the face? Do you feel foolish doing that? Why is it important to do it?

We receive grace to reign in life!

A king reigns in a nation, and as God's children, we are promised to reign in life! How do we reign? We can reign, or be victorious, only by His grace. We receive grace to reign in life...*those who receive God's abundant provision of grace and of the gift of righteousness reign in life through the one man, Jesus Christ (Romans 5:17).*

This promise is for all of us! Those who receive God's over-flowing grace and the free gift of righteousness will reign as kings in life. We are called to live above the circumstances, difficulties and problems because reigning comes from understanding the grace of God.

We can be victorious in every area of life—in our homes, in school, in our cell groups and churches and in our places of business. God has given us supernatural provision to live an overcomer's life. God gives us an abundance of grace! We do not deserve any of it, but the Lord pours it on us anyway!

Are you struggling with a habit that you have tried to break free from? Speak "Grace, grace" to it! Receive the divine energy that is needed to break free forever. Are you struggling in business, school or family relationships? Speak "Grace, grace" to the area of your life that seems like an impossible mountain to cross.

I had the privilege of addressing the students of Lifeway School in New Zealand where a proposed building project had come to a halt due to a lack of finances. Along with the students and the leadership of the school, we positioned ourselves toward the plot of land that was undeveloped and shouted, "Grace, grace." Within the next eight weeks, the school experienced a series of financial miracles, and the expansion of the facilities got underway. The only explanation was the grace of God!

REFLECTION
According to Romans 5:17, how do we get the power to reign as kings in this life? List struggles you are having, and shout "grace" to them. What do you expect to happen?

There are times when I'm speaking or counseling someone, and after I leave, I'll feel discouraged. Satan often tries to place condemnation on us so he can defeat us by capitalizing on the way we feel or the blunders we made. We must live by faith, not by our feelings. When things go bad, whether in our business, school, community, home, or church, we must never forget that God's grace gives us divine energy to push on through. When things are fine, we must not forget that it is only by God's grace that we are experiencing victory to reign in life!

God gives gifts according to grace

God's grace is so rich and multifaceted that a different aspect of it can be manifested through every believer. God gives gifts, inward motivations and abilities to believers so they may use them to benefit the rest of the body of Christ. These "grace gifts" are given to enable us to minister to others. *Having then gifts differing according to the grace that is given to us, let us use them...(Romans 12:6a NKJ)*

...If a man's gift is prophesying, let him use it in proportion to his faith. If it is serving, let him serve; if it is teaching, let him teach; if it is encouraging, let him encourage; if it is contributing to the needs of others, let him give generously; if it is leadership, let him govern diligently; if it is showing mercy, let him do it cheerfully (Romans 12:6b-8).

Have you ever witnessed to somebody and sensed the Holy Spirit moving through you as the right words came flowing from your mouth? This was simply the grace of God on your life as you shared the gospel. Do you enjoy serving? God has given you the desire and ability to give practical assistance to others. Teaching is the ability to examine God's Word and proclaim its truth so people grow in godliness. We should use the gift(s) to go about fulfilling God's purposes for our lives according to what He has given us. Each gift and ability that we have is a result of God's grace. He has given us these gifts and blessings in order to be a blessing and to serve others. *Each one should use whatever gift he has received to serve others, faithfully administering God's grace in its various forms (1 Peter 4:10).*

REFLECTION
What gifts has God given you to minister to others?
What gifts from God do others use to minister to you?

The gifts the Lord gives to us are divine abilities that we use to help and bless others. If you have the gift of prophecy, use it to speak encouragement and conviction in someone's life. If you have an inward motivation to give, those around you will be blessed by your financial help. When you operate in your gift(s), you are being used of the Lord to express His grace to others.

Comparing is not wise

Remember the grape-picking laborers in Matthew 20? They complained and wondered why everyone got paid the same for varying hours of labor because they didn't understand the grace of God. If we question why God gives some people greater talents and abilities than others, we have not understood the grace of God. If we think we are a better worship leader than Jim or a better teacher than Sally, we are falling short of God's grace.

It is so important to refrain from comparing ourselves with others. We should only compare ourselves with the Word of God and allow the Word to dwell in us so we can live out the principles of grace in our lives. If we feel like we are doing better than others, we fall into pride. If we feel like we are doing worse than those around us, we can suffer from feelings of inferiority. When we compare ourselves to others, we are not wise, according to God's Word in 2 Corinthians 10:12. *We do not dare to classify or compare ourselves with some who commend themselves. When they measure themselves by themselves and compare themselves with themselves, they are not wise.* Neither pride or inferiority are grace-filled responses.

REFLECTION
Do you feel better than other people you know? Worse? When we compare ourselves to others, what happens?

When God uses someone else for a certain ministry or responsibility and we are not called into action, how do we respond? When we begin to compare ourselves to other people, we are falling short of the grace of God. God is God. He knows best what we need. He may give somebody one gift and another a different type of gift. Understanding and walking in the grace of God will permeate our total being and way of thinking. It changes our attitudes, causing us to want to grow up spiritually so that we can help and serve those around us.

Impart grace to others

DAY 6

God has called you to impart His grace everywhere you go— work, school, home or to other believers in your small group. He has called you to impart grace to people and see them built up. *Do not let any unwholesome talk come out of your mouths, but only what is helpful for building others up according to their needs, that it may benefit those who listen (Ephesians 4:29).*

When we speak, we should say things that build people up so that we can impart grace (divine energy) into their lives. Words of encouragement will minister to others the grace that God has placed in our lives. When you thank your spouse, your parents or another family member, you are ministering the grace of God to them.

Thank your boss for his oversight at work. You are ministering the grace of God. Maybe you are a boss. You need to give encouragement to the people who work for you. You are ministering the grace of God to them.

Why not encourage your small group leader and minister grace to him or her? Encourage your leaders and thank them for what they have done. The grace of God should be the underlying attitude in everything we do. The book of Acts tells us that "much grace" was on the apostles. *With great power the apostles continued to testify to the resurrection of the Lord Jesus, and much grace was upon them all (Acts 4:33).*

We need a dose of God's "much grace" each day. John, the apostle, tells us that grace and truth come through Jesus Christ (John 1:17). Jesus has already granted us grace for our salvation. He is waiting for us to acknowledge Him and His grace so that we can experience His divine energy in our everyday living!

REFLECTION
Describe a time you imparted grace into someone's life. Did you see immediate results or not?

Why should we be careful not to allow discouraging words to come out of our mouths? Think of some people to whom the Lord may be asking you to minister His grace today, and do it!

All credit to God

We will never take credit for what God does if we understand His grace. For example, I have had the privilege of ministering to many people throughout the world in the past few years. It has been such a blessing to see people's lives changed by the power of God. I could never take credit for that. I know it is only by the grace of God I can minister the good news of Jesus Christ.

The Bible tells us we are all competent ministers (2 Corinthians 3:5); we are called to help other people and minister in Jesus' name. It's not us ministering to others in our own strength, but God who lives inside of us ministering through us. You and I are called to be channels of God's love.

Electric wire is a channel for electric power. We don't see an electric line and think, "What a beautiful wire." No, we are just thankful for the power that comes through the wire. Likewise, we are channels of the Holy Spirit, and we can never take credit for anything that God does. We must allow His grace and power to flow from our lives. We have been chosen as heirs of Christ to carry His banner because...*having been justified by his grace, we might become heirs having the hope of eternal life (Titus 3:7).* What an awesome privilege—of all the people in the world, He has chosen you and me!

I encourage you to begin to shout "Grace, grace" to the mountains in your life. Remember Zerubbabel? He knew that the grace of God would be released and the people would get the job completed quickly, effectively and efficiently if he was obedient. So the people shouted, "Grace, grace" to the temple, and it was completed, causing great excitement among the people. They realized that it wasn't their strength but the strength of God's grace working through them.

No matter what situation you find yourself in, you need to learn to speak "Grace, grace" to it. If you have a habit you want to conquer, but have repeatedly fallen flat on your face, begin to speak "grace" to that situation. Maybe you are a businessman and struggling financially. Begin to speak grace to your business. Perhaps you are encouraging a new believer who is dealing with some area of his or her life. Begin to speak grace to that area. Is there a conflict in your marriage? Maybe you are a single person and have a special need. Begin to speak grace to your life. Maybe your prayer life needs revitalizing. Speak grace to your prayer life.

The commander in chief of the armies of heaven is waiting for us to declare "Grace, grace" over our families, our churches, our cities and our nations. The kingdoms of this world shall become the kingdoms of our Lord and of His Christ, and He shall reign forever and ever! (Revelation 11:15).

REFLECTION
List areas of your life that need grace applied to them.

"Grace, grace!"

CHAPTER 4

Grace for Everyday Living

KEY MEMORY VERSE

But grow in the grace and knowledge
of our Lord and Savior Jesus Christ.
To him be glory both now and forever! Amen.
2 Peter 3:18

Grow in grace

When I was young in the Lord, I did not understand grace at all. I thought God really owed me something. "Look, God," I said, "I've given you my life. I've given you everything. I've given you my family. It all belongs to you." I was working sixty hours on a job in addition to being involved with a full-time youth ministry. I thought, "God, you have to take care of my family. You have to take care of my relationship with my wife. After all, I'm serving you; I'm giving you my life." I later realized that God didn't owe me anything. God did not owe me a strong marriage or a healthy family. But even though I did not deserve it, God wanted to give me a strong marriage and family because of His awesome grace. Praise God for His grace!

The grace of God will affect every area of your life. We can do absolutely nothing except by the grace of God. Do we deserve a bright, sunny, summer day? No. But we receive the sunshine because of the grace of God. We stand in a position for the sun to shine on us, and when we see the sun, we receive it. As Christians, we need to get into a position to receive the grace of God in our lives. However, growing in grace is a process. It doesn't just happen overnight. *But grow in the grace and knowledge of our Lord and Savior Jesus Christ. To him be glory both now and forever! Amen (2 Peter 3:18).*

God gives us grace to grow every step of the way if we walk in obedience to Him. We were saved because of God's grace through faith (Ephesians 2:5,8) and we continue to receive grace to live the

REFLECTION
Does God owe us anything because we serve Him? Tell of ways you have grown in the grace of God.

Christian life. In this chapter, we will look at several areas in our daily lives that God wants to invade and keep permeating with His grace.

The fruit of the Spirit

How, then, do we grow in grace? The Spirit and our sinful nature are at war with each other. Since the sinful nature remains within us after our conversion and is our deadly enemy (Romans 8:6-8,13; Galatians 5:17,21), it must be resisted and put to death in a continual warfare that we wage through the power of the Holy Spirit (Romans 8:4-14). If we do not fight a battle against our sinful nature and continue to practice the acts of the sinful nature, the Bible says we cannot inherit God's kingdom (Galatians 5:21). According to Galatians 5:19-21, our sinful nature causes us to fall into such terrible things as sexual immorality, impurity, debauchery, idolatry, witchcraft, hatred, discord, jealousy, fits of rage, selfish ambition, dissensions, factions, envy, drunkenness and orgies.

Thank God for His grace because this list of the acts of our sinful nature in Galatians continues on to say that when we fellowship with God, He produces the fruit of the Spirit in our lives. *But the fruit of the Spirit is love, joy, peace, patience, kindness, goodness, faithfulness, gentleness and self-control...Those who belong to Christ Jesus have crucified the sinful nature with its passions and desires. Since we live by the Spirit, let us keep in step with the Spirit. The contrast between the life-style of the Spirit-filled Christian and one who is controlled by his sinful nature is clear. Our human nature with its corrupt desires is our "sinful nature" (Galatians 5:22-26).*

When we depend on God's grace to live a life-style of love, joy, peace, patience, kindness, goodness, faithfulness, gentleness and self-control, we will experience these virtues or "fruits" in our lives. When we allow the Holy Spirit to direct our lives, sin's power is destroyed. We can then walk in fellowship with God, and by His grace, He will produce the fruit of the Spirit to help us live victoriously in every area of our lives.

REFLECTION
What happens to our sinful nature when we begin to fellowship with God (Galatians 5:22-26)? How does the fruit of the Spirit cause us to grow in grace?

Grace to live sexually pure

Standards for sexual morality are clear in God's Word. Believers must live morally and sexually pure lives, according to Hebrews 13:4. *Marriage should be honored by all, and the marriage bed kept pure, for God will judge the adulterer and all the sexually immoral.*

The word *pure* in the Greek means *to be free from all that which is lewd.* It suggests refraining from all acts and thoughts that incite desire not in accordance with one's virginity or one's marriage vows. It stresses restraint and avoidance of all sexual actions and excitements that would defile our purity before God. It includes controlling our own bodies "in a way that is holy and honorable" (1

Thessalonians 4:4), and not in "passionate lust" (4:5). This scriptural instruction is for both those who are single and those who are married.[1]

Sexual intimacy has boundaries. It is reserved for the marriage relationship when a man and a woman become one. In that arena, God blesses the relationship with the physical and emotional pleasures that result.

Premarital sex is condemned in the Bible. Self-control is a fruit of the Spirit that contrasts with getting involved in sexual gratification with someone who is not one's marriage partner...*Do not arouse or awaken love until it so desires (Song of Songs 2:7).* This phrase occurs two more times in the Song of Songs (3:5; 8:4) where the Shulammite woman says she does not want physical intimacy until she and Solomon are married. Virginity until marriage is God's sexual standard of purity for men and women.

What about homosexuality? Homosexuality has become a huge issue in modern culture. Homosexual or gay persons have often been excluded and persecuted by a culture that hypocritically glorifies other forms of sexual sin. A gay person should not be treated differently from those who have fallen victim to other types of sin. Homosexual practice is sin (Romans 1:26-27; 1 Timothy 1:9-10), but sin is by no means unique to homosexuals. We are all sinners. Paul's words in 1 Corinthians 6:9-11 describe homosexuality as a sin, but he calls upon Christians to treat the homosexual as a person who is in need of forgiveness and transformation. *Do you not know that the wicked will not inherit the kingdom of God? Do not be deceived: Neither the sexually immoral nor idolaters nor adulterers nor male prostitutes nor homosexual offenders nor thieves nor the greedy nor drunkards nor slanderers nor swindlers will inherit the kingdom of God. And that is what some of you were. But you were washed, you were sanctified, you were justified in the name of the Lord Jesus Christ and by the Spirit of our God.*

Sometimes Christians continue to struggle with same sex attraction. Understanding and wise guidance can make the difference in helping those attracted to the

REFLECTION
Why is it important to live a sexually pure life (Hebrews 13:4)?
Is homosexuality a sin (1 Corinthians 6:9-11)?

Biblical Foundations

same sex to avoid homosexual activity altogether. Both those who are tempted and those who are already caught in sin (Galatians 6:1) need to be restored in a spirit of compassion and gentleness. As Christians, we must be ministers of God's transforming grace toward homosexuals and those struggling with its temptations. The Bible provides hope for every sinner. Everyone is equally in need of God's grace. We must love people as we point them toward the victorious life that is possible through Jesus Christ.

[1] *Full Life Study Bible*, (Grand Rapids, Michigan: Zondervan Publishing House, 1992), p. 1936.

Grace for marriage

Marriage is God's idea. Genesis 2:24 implies that marriage is an exclusive relationship (a man...his wife), which is publicly acknowledged (leaves his parents), permanent (cleaves to his wife), and consummated by having sexual relations (they will become one flesh). The marriage bond is a divine covenant that is intended to last for life. Fidelity, support and mutual sharing as the husband and wife build the life of Christ in each other are at the center of the relationship.

God gave man rulership over every living creature (Genesis 1:28). He then placed man in the Garden of Eden to care for His creation (Genesis 2:15). He created order so that things would not be in chaos in the world. The same is true of marriage. The scriptural basis for order in Christian marriage is found in Ephesians 5:21-33. *Submit to one another out of reverence for Christ. Wives, submit to your husbands as to the Lord. For the husband is the head of the wife as Christ is the head of the church, his body, of which he is the Savior...In this same way, husbands ought to love their wives as their own bodies. He who loves his wife loves himself. After all, no one ever hated his own body, but he feeds and cares for it, just as Christ does the church—for we are members of his body. "For this reason a man will leave his father and mother and be united to his wife, and the two will become one flesh." This is a profound mystery—but I am talking about Christ and the church. However, each one of you also must love his wife as he loves himself, and the wife must respect her husband.*

Husbands and wives need to submit to each other in love. This scripture says that the husband is positionally the "head" of the wife which means he is the responsible one. Responsibility, however, does not mean control. In today's world where domestic violence is a huge problem, we can never think that physical or verbal abuse is about a lack of submission. Selfishness and control is not a form of headship. Any kind of abuse in marriage, including physical, emotional, spiritual or sexual is wrong. If physical abuse occurs, a spouse should seek a safe place.

Marriage is instituted by God so that men and women can mutually complete each other. Marriage takes two people, working hard at nourishing this bond. Sadly, in today's world, the incidence of divorce has reached epidemic proportions. What about a marriage that has failed? Read the next section for some answers.

REFLECTION
How much should a husband love his wife, according to Ephesians 5:21-33?
How does a wife "submit to her husband as to the Lord"?

Grace when a marriage fails

Reconciliation lies at the very heart of Christianity. Although scripture cites two biblical grounds for divorce, every effort should be made to restore a marriage. Paul, the apostle wrote to the Corinthian church, *Are you married? Do not seek a divorce...(1 Corinthians 7:27a).*

When the Pharisees asked Jesus about the grounds for divorce, He referred them to the original institution of marriage (Matthew 19:3-8) stressing that marriage is intended for life. God hates divorce (Malachi 2:13-16). Divorce is devastating. It has an effect, not on just two people, but their children and families. Reconciliation in marriage is God's desire (1 Corinthians 7:12-14). However, sometimes reconciliation is not possible. In this case, God's Word cites two reasons when divorce is permitted—for marital unfaithfulness (Matthew 5:31-32; 19:9) or abandonment (1 Corinthians 7:15-16).

Failure in marriage often has *selfishness* as its roots. We want what we want! Regardless of the reasons, we have to face the facts: today's world is full of broken marriages. We must minister with compassion to those facing a failed marriage.

Those going through a divorce have experienced a breakdown in trust. At this crucial and heartbreaking time, a person going through a divorce needs prayerful accountability with trusted church leadership or counselors. They will need to deal with trust and fear issues (How can I ever trust a spouse again? What will keep another marriage from failing?).

Some of the most heroic people are those who have been sinned against by having to experience abandonment, separation, and/or divorce unwillingly. These persons have not sinned, but feel rejected by many in the church today. Jesus does not abandon, separate from (reject), or divorce those who are His. During these times, His grace will increase! *Marriage should be honored by all, and the marriage bed kept pure, for God will judge the adulterer and all the*

REFLECTION
How can we minister with compassion to a person going through a divorce?
Who will never leave us, according to Hebrews 13:4-6?

sexually immoral...God has said, "Never will I leave you; never will I forsake you." So we say with confidence, "The Lord is my helper; I will not be afraid. What can man do to me?" (Hebrews 13:4-6).

Grace for singles

DAY 6

We said earlier that sex is for marriage only. What does the Bible say about singleness? The world may say that a human cannot live without sexual experience but the Bible disagrees. A single person can be fulfilled and live without sexual experience. Jesus referred to singleness as a divine vocation in Matthew 19:12. *Others have renounced marriage because of the kingdom of heaven. The one who can accept this should accept it.*

The apostle Paul said that one of the blessings of singleness is that it releases people to give their undivided devotion to Jesus. *I would like you to be free from concern. An unmarried man is concerned about the Lord's affairs—how he can please the Lord. But a married man is concerned about the affairs of this world-how he can please his wife—and his interests are divided. An unmarried woman or virgin is concerned about the Lord's affairs: Her aim is to be devoted to the Lord in both body and spirit. But a married woman is concerned about the affairs of this world—how she can please her husband. I am saying this for your own good, not to restrict you, but that you may live in a right way in undivided devotion to the Lord (1 Corinthians 7:32-35).*

He also says that both singleness and marriage are a gift of God's grace. *I wish that all men were as I am. But each man has his own gift from God; one has this gift, another has that (1 Corinthians 7:7).* Both the married person and unmarried will receive grace for the state in which they find themselves.

Unmarried people may be quite lonely at times, but God always gives the grace to live in obedience to Him. If you're single, you are not half a person. You are whole in Christ. He wants you to be fulfilled as a single person, and He will give you the grace.

REFLECTION
What is an advantage of being single, according to 1 Corinthians 7:32-35?

Grace is available; don't miss it!

The writer of Hebrews 12:15 warns believers that they should not miss God's grace. *See to it that no one misses the grace of God....* We can miss God's grace when we try to live the Christian life by our own efforts. In Galatians 5:3-4, Paul says the Galatians had moved from a faith in Christ to legalistic observances of the law. Thus, they had...*fallen away from grace (v.5).*

Sometimes people say of someone who hurt them, "He really hurt my feelings." If we allow our hurt feelings to control our lives, we are not living in the realm of God's grace. Who says everyone should be nice to us? If we are misunderstood, the only reason it is not much worse is because of the grace of God. If we are hurt, we are demanding our own rights. But we do not have rights. They were nailed to the cross two thousand years ago. We no longer have a *right* to not get hurt. However, we do have *privileges* whereby we can live for God and experience a victorious life. These privileges we have are the result of the grace of God.

Let it be clear that as Christians we do have rights against the devil. The Bible teaches us that we have spiritual rights as we stand against the devil to rebuke him in the name of Jesus. We have the right to use the name of Jesus and the blood of Christ and the Word of God. But we need to realize that even that right is available because of the grace of God.

Often when I meet parents who have raised godly families, I ask them, "How did you do it?" I have not been surprised by their answer. They tell me it was simply the grace of God. If we think we deserve godly children, a good job and good friends because we have done all the right things, we are simply wrong!

I am thankful that God has given me a wonderful family and marriage. But it is not because of anything that I have done. I am simply a recipient of the grace of God that I have received from Him as a free gift.

From start to finish, we must live our lives in God's grace. God's grace through faith brings salvation to us at the start of our Christian lives and continues giving us the power and ability to respond to God and resist sin. Grace is a wonderful gift that God gives because He loves us!

REFLECTION

How can we miss the grace of God? Explain the difference between having rights and privileges.

What Is Grace?

1. Grace affects everything

Ex: Bear in a metal and mental prison cannot change, even when given the opportunity.

a. Like the bear, some Christians are so accustomed to thought patterns of defeat and failure, they are locked in an invisible prison.

b. We receive grace freely and do not deserve it, and our hearts cannot but change because of it!

c. Grace is mentioned more than 125 times in the New Testament. Paul often began his letters speaking about grace (1 Corinthians 1:3-4).

2. God's free gift of grace is the basis of salvation

a. Grace is defined as the *free unmerited favor of God on the undeserving and ill-deserving.*

b. Our first glimpse of grace occurs at salvation (Ephesians 2:8-9). God draws us (John 6:44).

c. It is grace that motivates God to offer us salvation even though we did not earn it (Romans 11:6).

d. Two sides of grace: the saving grace of God "the free unmerited favor of God" and the grace God gives to believers to give them "a desire and power to do God's will" (we look at this concept in Chapters 3-4).

3. Mercy vs. grace

a. Mercy is "God not giving us what we deserve" and grace is "God giving us those things we do not deserve."

Ex: Police officer giving speeding ticket with various scenarios.

b. If we think God owes us something, we are not operating in grace.

4. No longer under the law but under grace

a. God gave Moses moral laws to follow (Ten Commandments) which showed mankind their sinful condition as they attempted to obey the law.

b. Jesus changed all that. Through Him we are offered grace— our righteousness no longer depends on keeping the law (John 1:17).

c. Those under the law are always conscious of it. To escape dominion of sin, a Christian comes out from under the law and comes under grace (Romans 6:14).

5. The Ten Commandments show how important grace is

Deuteronomy 5:6-21

a. Discuss the Ten Commandments and your inability to keep them.

b. The Ten Commandments convince us of our sinfulness and inability to keep the law. Sin has no dominion over us because we are not under the law, but under grace!

6. Grace is more powerful than sin

a. The more we see the extent of our failure to obey God's laws, the more we see God's grace toward us.

Romans 5:20

b. The Holy Spirit works in believers to allow them to live lives of righteousness, only by God's grace!

7. Cheap grace?

a. Can we depend on God's forgiveness of sin and continue to sin and remain secure from judgment? (Romans 6:1)

b. We must be careful to daily reaffirm our decision to resist sin and follow Christ (Romans 8:13; Hebrews 3:7-11).

c. If we cease to resist sin, eventually our hearts grow hard. It is possible to become sin's slave again with death as its result (Romans 6:23).

Responding to God's Grace

1. Totally dependent on God's grace

a. Apostle Paul had all the advantages of birth, education and personal achievement. Yet he attributed it all to the grace of God (1 Corinthians 15:10).

b. Every good thing in our lives comes because of the grace of God.

2. God gives us unlimited grace to change

a. We should not be passive about desiring and accepting grace.

b. Take God at His Word and trust His grace to see things changed in our lives and live victoriously. He gives more grace (James 4:6).

c. Continue in His grace even in opposition (Acts 13:43).

3. Falling short of God's grace

a. Parable of landowner with vineyard (Matthew 20:11-15). We must live completely satisfied, not concerned if someone gets a better deal than we do.

b. We will not grow bitter or jealous when we live in the grace of God (Hebrews 12:15).

4. Grace to the humble

a. Humility is an attitude of dependence on Jesus Christ. 1 Peter 5:5-6

b. Humility places us in a position to receive God's grace.

5. Season your speech with grace

a. Our words should be seasoned with grace (Colossians 4:6).
   Ex: Liver seasoned the right way can be edible!

b. How we say something is as important as what we say, especially when we give a word of correction to someone. Ephesians 4:15

6. God's grace through suffering

a. There are many reasons why we suffer as a consequence of our actions, because we live in a sinful world, demonic affliction, etc.

b. Being faithful to God does not guarantee we will be free from pain and suffering in this life but we will not be "tempted beyond what we can bear" (1 Corinthians 10:13).

d. Suffering often opens us up to God's abundant grace. 2 Corinthians 12:9; Jeremiah 31:2

e. In the midst of sufferings in life, we are sustained by an inner life that cannot be defeated (2 Corinthians 4:7-8).

7. Allow His grace to motivate you

a. Even in bad days, we should give thanks. 1 Thessalonians 5:18

b. We should not take God's grace for granted. 2 Corinthians 6:1-2

c. If we find ourselves outside of the grace of God, we are urged to be reconciled (2 Corinthians 5:20).

Speaking Grace to the Mountain

1. Grace releases divine energy

a. The other side of grace: the power and desire to do God's will. God's grace releases divine energy in our lives.

Ex: The Lord gives divine energy to complete the work on the temple (Zechariah 4:6-7) as they shouted "grace" to the project.

b. Shout "grace" to the mountain of impossibility before you and find your focus changing from your ability (or lack) to His ability.

2. Speak grace to impossible situations

a. The wisdom of God and the wisdom of the world are at odds (1 Corinthians 1:18). The world's wisdom emphasizes our ability to take care of ourselves while God's wisdom emphasizes complete dependence on Him.

Ex: Exodus 17: Why did army advance only when Moses arms were held up? Made no sense to the natural mind.

b. If the Lord instructs us to do something, we should be obedient (2 Kings 13:19). Why is it important to be obedient?

3. We receive grace to reign in life!

a. We receive grace to reign in life (Romans 5:17). We can live above our circumstances and difficulties and receive grace to live victoriously.

b. Speak "grace, grace" to an area in your life that seems like an impossible mountain to cross. What do you expect to happen?

4. God gives gifts according to grace
a. God gives gifts (inward motivations and abilities) to believers to benefit the body of Christ.
b. These "grace gifts" are used to minister to others (Romans 12:6-8) and serve them (1 Peter 4:10).

5. Comparing is not wise
a. We should not compare ourselves with others but with the Word of God.
b. Neither pride or inferiority are grace-filled responses. 2 Corinthians 10:12
c. When we compare ourselves to others, what happens?

6. Impart grace to others
a. Impart divine energy to others with our speech. Ephesians 4:29
b. We need a dose of much grace (Acts 4:33) just as the apostles had.

7. All credit to God
a. We are all competent ministers (2 Corinthians 3:5) and God lives inside, ministering through us.

   Ex: Electric wire is a channel for power just as we are channels for God's grace and power to flow through us.
b. We are heirs of Christ, justified by His grace (Titus 3:7).
c. Shout "grace, grace" to mountains of impossibility in your life.

Grace for Everyday Living

1. Grow in grace
a. Grace of God affects every area of our lives.
b. God gives us grace to grow spiritually (2 Peter 3:18).
c. We are saved by grace (Ephesians 2:5,8) and continue to receive grace to live the Christian life.

2. The fruit of the Spirit
a. Our sinful nature must be resisted in a continual warfare we wage through the power of the Holy Spirit (Romans 8:4-14).
b. Thank God for grace because when we fellowship with God, He produces the fruit of the Spirit in our lives (Galatians 5:22-26). When we allow the Holy Spirit to direct our lives, sin's power is destroyed so we can live victoriously.

3. Grace to live sexually pure
a. Believers must live sexually pure lives (Hebrews 13:4). Pure means controlling our bodies in a way that is holy and honorable (1 Thessalonians 4:4-5).
b. Sexual intimacy has boundaries—reserved for the marriage relationship. Premarital sex is condemned.
c. Homosexuality is sin (1 Corinthians 6:9-11; Romans 1:26-27). We must help believers struggling with same-sex attraction and point them toward the victorious life possible through Jesus Christ.

4. Grace for marriage

a. Marriage is an exclusive relationship between a man and a woman (Genesis 2:24).

b. There is order in nature and also in marriage: Ephesians 5:21-33—Husbands and wives submit to each other, with the husband positionally the head of his wife. He is the responsible one.

c. Marriage takes two people, working hard to nourish the bond.

5. Grace when a marriage fails

a. Every effort should be made to restore a failing marriage.

b. Two grounds for divorce: marital unfaithfulness or abandonment (Matthew 5:31-32; 19:9; 1 Corinthians 7:15-16).

c. A person going through divorce needs prayerful accountability. God's grace will increase in a time of need. He will never forsake us (Hebrews 13:4-6).

6. Grace for singles

a. Apostle Paul said one blessing of singleness is that it releases the individual to give his undivided devotion to Jesus (1 Corinthians 7:32-35).

b. Both marriage and singleness are a gift of God's grace and both receive grace for the state in which they find themselves (1 Corinthians 7:7).

7. Grace is available; don't miss it!

a. Grace can be missed according to Hebrews 12:15. When we try to live by our own efforts, we are missing God's grace (Galatians 5:3-4).

b. Living in God's grace means we cannot demand our rights. We have only privileges as a result of the grace of God.

c. From start to finish, our lives must be lived in God's grace.

Chapter 1
What is Grace?
Journaling space for reflection questions

DAY 1

Like the bear in the cage, are you held captive to any old habits or deceptions?

DAY 2

How does grace first impact our lives according to Ephesians 2:8-9? Describe the two sides of grace.

DAY 3

What are some things God gave you because of His grace? What are some things He did not give because of His mercy?

DAY 4 *The law came through Moses, but what came through Jesus Christ according to John 1:17? How do we escape the law and come under grace?*

DAY 5 *Think about your life and your inability to keep the ten commandments. How important is grace to your life?*

DAY 6 *What increases with sin, according to Romans 5:20? How have you experienced this in your life?*

DAY 7 *Since grace increases with sin, can we continue to sin because God will always forgive us? What can happen if we keep returning to sin, according to Romans 6:23?*

Living in the Grace of God

Chapter 2
Responding to God's Grace
Journaling space for reflection questions

DAY 1 *Can you honestly agree with the following statements? I am totally dependent on the grace of God. I am what I am by the grace of God.*

DAY 2 *Describe a time you received grace to live victoriously.*

DAY 3 *What is a "root of bitterness," according to Hebrews 12:15? Does it ever cause trouble in your life?*

According to 1 Peter 5:5-6, how can we humble ourselves?

Tell about a time you spoke words "full of grace, seasoned with salt" into someone's life. What were the results?

How does suffering and grace work together, according to 2 Corinthians 12:9?

What can happen when we "receive God's grace in vain"? How are we reconciled back to God (2 Corinthians 5:20)?

Chapter 3
Speaking Grace to the Mountain
Journaling space for reflection questions

DAY 1

Explain "divine energy." How is it at work in your life?

DAY 2

How does God respond to our shouting "grace, grace" to the mountains of impossibility that stare us in the face? Do you feel foolish doing that? Why is it important to do it?

DAY 3

According to Romans 5:17, how do we get the power to reign as kings in this life? List struggles you are having, and shout "grace" to them. What do you expect to happen?

DAY 4

What gifts has God given you to minister to others?
What gifts from God do others use to minister to you?

DAY 5

Do you feel better than other people you know? Worse?
When we compare ourselves to others, what happens?

DAY 6

Describe a time you imparted grace into someone's life.
Did you see immediate results or not?

DAY 7

List areas of your life that need grace applied to them.

Chapter 4
Grace for Everyday Living
Journaling space for reflection questions

Does God owe us anything because we serve Him?
Tell of ways you have grown in the grace of God.

What happens to our sinful nature when we begin to fellowship
with God (Galatians 5:22-26)?
How does the fruit of the Spirit cause us to grow in grace?

Why is it important to live a sexually pure life (Hebrews 13:4)?
Is homosexuality a sin (1 Corinthians 6:9-11)?

Biblical Foundations

DAY 4 *How much should a husband love his wife, according to Ephesians 5:21-33? How does a wife "submit to her husband as to the Lord"?*

DAY 5 *How can we minister with compassion to a person going through a divorce? Who will never leave us, according to Hebrews 13:4-6?*

DAY 6 *What is an advantage of being single, according to 1 Corinthians 7:32-35?*

DAY 7 *How can we miss the grace of God?*
Explain the difference between having rights and privileges.

Daily Devotional Extra Days

If you are using this book as a daily devotional, you will notice there are 28 days in this study. Depending on the month, you may need the three extra days' studies given here.

DAY 29 — Dead to Sin

Read Romans 6:1-2,11-12. Since sin is rampant in the world, and since grace is greater than sin, should you sin so that God pours out more grace? Explain. Have you died to sin or are you still a slave to sin? What does the Bible tell us to do about sin that would try to creep into our lives?

DAY 30 — Grace and Humility

Read Romans 12:3. Paul is writing to the church at Rome and admits that it is only through God's grace that he instructs them in humility. As Christ increases in you, you will decrease. This is the opposite of pride (which elevates self over God). How do you judge yourself to be in relation to others? How does the Lord want us to see ourselves?

DAY 31 — God's Grace in Your Life

Read Romans 16:20,24. Can you completely trust God's power to defeat your enemies? Do you believe that God's grace is over your life as a believer in Christ Jesus? Explain. Receive God's grace when it is spoken over you, and, in turn, speak it over the lives of others.

Coordinates with this series!

Biblical Foundations for Children

Creative learning experiences for ages 4-12, patterned after the *Biblical Foundation Series*, with truths in each lesson. Takes kids on the first steps in their Christian walk by teaching them how to build solid foundations in their young lives. by Jane Nicholas, 176 pages: $17.95 ISBN:1-886973-35-0

Other books by Larry Kreider

House to House

The church is waking up to the simple, successful house to house strategy practiced by the New Testament church. *House to House* documents how God called a small fellowship of believers to become a house to house movement. During the past years, DOVE Christian Fellowship Int'l has grown into a family of cell-based churches and house churches networking throughout the world. by Larry Kreider, 206 pages: $8.95 ISBN:1-880828-81-2

The Cry for Spiritual Fathers & Mothers

Returning to the biblical truth of spiritual parenting so believers are not left fatherless and disconnected. How loving, seasoned spiritual fathers and mothers help spiritual children reach their full potential in Christ. by Larry Kreider, 186 pages: $11.95 ISBN:1-886973-42-3

Helping You Build Cell Churches

A complete biblical blueprint for small group ministry, this comprehensive manual covers 54 topics! Gives full, integrated training to build cell churches from the ground up. Compiled by Brian Sauder and Larry Kreider, 256 pages: $19.95 ISBN:1-886973-38-5

Check our Web site:
www.dcfi.org

DOVE Christian Fellowship International presents

Hearing God 30 Different Ways Seminar
Learn to "tune in" to God and discern "HIS" voice. God wants to speak to you. Each attendee receives a seminar manual.

Spiritual Fathering & Mothering Seminar
Practical preparation for believers who want to have and become spiritual parents. Each attendee receives a seminar manual.

Elder's and Church Leadership Training
Based on New Testament leadership principles, this seminar equips leaders to provide protection, direction and correction in the local church. Each attendee receives a seminar manual.

Small Groups 101 Seminar
Basics for healthy cell ministry. Session topics cover the essentials for growing cell group ministry. Each attendee receives a *Helping You Build* Manual.

Small Groups 201 Seminar
Takes you beyond the basics and into an advanced strategy for cell ministry. Each attendee receives a seminar manual.

Counseling Basics
This seminar takes you through the basics of counseling, specifically in small group ministry. Includes a comprehensive manual.

Marriage Mentoring Training Seminar
Trains church leaders and mature believers to help prepare engaged couples for a strong marriage foundation by using the mentoring format of *Called Together*. Includes a *Called Together Manual*.

**For additional seminars
and more information
www.dcfi.org
Call 800.848.5892
email: info@dcfi.org**